T0069204

ZEUS
and the
GIANT
ICED
TEA

Mingling Voices

Series editor: Manijeh Mannani

Give us wholeness, for we are broken.
But who are we asking, and why do we ask?
— Phyllis Webb

National in scope, *Mingling Voices* draws on the work of both new and established novelists, short story tellers, and poets. The series especially, but not exclusively, aims to promote authors who challenge traditions and cultural stereotypes. It is designed to reach a wide variety of readers, both generalists and specialists. *Mingling Voices* is also open to literary works that delineate the immigrant experience in Canada.

Series Titles

Poems for a Small Park
by E.D. Blodgett

Dreamwork
by Jonathan Locke Hart

Windfall Apples: Tanka and Kyoka
by Richard Stevenson

The dust of just beginning
by Don Kerr

Roy & Me: This Is Not a Memoir
by Maurice Yacowar

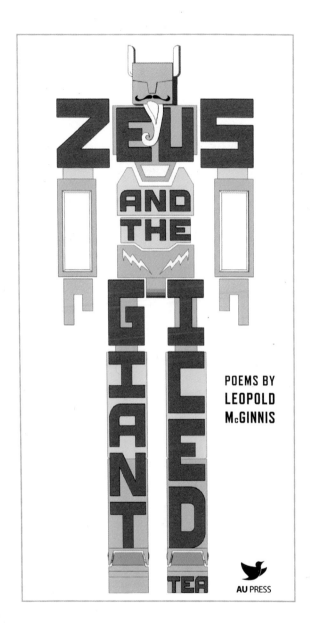

ZEUS AND THE GIANT ICED TEA

POEMS BY
LEOPOLD
McGINNIS

AU PRESS

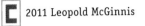
Published by AU Press, Athabasca University
1200, 10011 – 109 Street
Edmonton, AB T5J 3S8

Library and Archives Canada Cataloguing in Publication

McGinnis, Leopold, 1977–
Zeus and the giant iced tea / by Leopold McGinnis.

(Mingling voices series, ISSN 1917-9405)
Poems.
Also issued in electronic format (ISBN 978-1-897425-95-4).
ISBN 978-1-897425-94-7

I. Title.
II. Series: Mingling voices

PS8625.G56Z49 2011   C811'.6   C2010-907660-5

Cover and book design by Natalie Olsen, Kisscut Design.
Printed and bound in Canada by Marquis Book Printing.

We acknowledge the financial support of the Government
of Canada through the Canada Book Fund (CBF) for our
publishing activities. ▐✦▐ Canadian Heritage   Patrimoine canadien

A volume in the Mingling Voices series:
ISSN 1917-9405 (Print)   ISSN 1917-9413 (Online)

for mama

simply,
thanks

Why ZEUS AND THE GIANT ICED TEA?

This is the story about a series of stories.

I don't write poems for publication. I just write them. For myself, typically. So when it comes down to having to assemble all your eating-Wheaties-at-breakfast poems, your depressed-out-of-your-little-pea-sized-brain poems, your god-damn-I'm-horny-as-hell-poems and your hey-wouldn't-it-be-cool-to-write-a-poem-about-this? poems into a cohesive collection, well... how do you go about that exactly?

It's not so easy. Maybe some artists (and I know some like this) can just grab a handful out of a drawer, pop 'em in a whirlyque, spin 'em around, collate them and voilà! *Une collection*. But I'm way too anal for that.

My first collection of poems wasn't so bad to assemble... thanks to lack of experience. I'd never expected my poetry to find publication in book form. Considering how underwhelmingly my fictional work fared, it was just too unlikely for me to entertain much fantasy on the subject of a *published* book of poetry. And yet, through some coalescence of connections, luck, hard work, and (dare I say it?) talent, I found myself having to put together my first collection of poems.

But, like I said, that wasn't too bad. I saw *Poetaster*, my first book, as an introduction to me and my work. As such, I just gathered up all my poems and picked out eighty I liked the best, keeping some eye to how they worked together. *Poetaster* was essentially a thematic sampling of the diverse sort of work I'd done up to that point. A "Hello World" grab bag. That was the "concept."

But what to do when you're asked to put together a SECOND collection? I didn't really want to do "Random Poetry by Leopold McGinnis, Part 2." I'd introduced myself; now I had to do something different. You know... razzle-dazzle 'em. But how? After my first publication I'd started looking at poetry books in a different way. Not just in passive enjoyment, but more in a "Why did they pick these poems, and how did they organize them together?" spirit. There were plenty of random collections, but I grew increasingly intrigued by the books that presented a number of poems strung together by some common thread. I liked the idea of doing an entire collection on one theme... but because of the vagrant nature of my writing I wasn't sure I had enough poetry on any one topic to make a book. And a not-so-quick hands-on assessment proved I was correct on that front.

(I'm getting to the "why this book is called *Zeus and the Giant Iced Tea*" bit. Just bear with me for a sec.)

But as I was slogging through my stuff I realized that I had quite a number of poems that were not thematically similar but formatically similar, to invent a word. Narratives! They were all aiming to tell a story of some kind, in their own interesting and unusual ways. Even better, when joined together, they formed a sort of Voltron team of poetics — their collective grouping bringing something new to the poems themselves, adding layers of meaning and excellent other powers that I couldn't take credit for creating. Shouldn't any good collection raise the individual pieces within to higher levels, open up a new horizon of understanding above and beyond the parts? What good is a giant robot if you can't combine that giant robot with six other giant robots to create a super giant robot? Not much, I tell you!

The interesting thing for me about this collection is what it explores in terms of the narrative format both intentionally and unintentionally. These are all story-structured poems. However, together they take us on a tour through a zoo of forms. Some poems here are almost short stories in poetry format. In "The Secret," I could be accused of just taking a short story and inserting copious line breaks. Others are autobiographical — "The Big Shot," for instance. Some are realistic, many are dreamlike. Some follow a traditional narrative structure of beginning, middle, end, moral. Others just hint at a brief piece of a bigger story. Despite all being poems, they represent a wide variety of stories and ways of telling a story. None of these poems aims to talk about narratives or ostensibly play with the narrative format. And yet, as a group, they do. I like that. It's like a poetry playground — put 'em together and see how it comes out.

Even more interesting, this collection posed to me the question: "When is a narrative a narrative?" That is, how do you decide when a poem is a narrative? Even a plotless poem about feeling sad is on some level a story, whether explicit or not. A descriptive poem about a flower implies a story. Why this flower?

Where is it? Why is the poet driven to talk about this flower? So when it came time to start deciding what did and did not qualify for *Zeus,* I had to make tough decisions. "The Secret" obviously qualifies...but poems like "Who's going to fulfill my unreasonable expectations?" and "The Last Generation" were not so cut-and-dried. There are no obvious story lines there...Anyway, I put a lot of thought into this, and in the end, for one reason or another, I decided that all the poems in this book met the criteria, however vague, for narrative. This in itself was a fun exercise, and perhaps one the reader might find entertaining to consider while reading through the collection.

Which brings me to why this collection is called *Zeus and the Giant Iced Tea*. Mostly it's because I needed a name for the collection, and *Zeus and the Giant Iced Tea* was the poem title that, if put on the cover of a book, seemed most likely to encourage someone to pick the book up and take a look. I mean...that would grab *my* attention! But I also feel that the poems in this collection sort of follow Zeus's dreamy train of thought in that poem. These poems move from one kind of story to the next, as one thought might move to the next in a daydream. There's no wholesale conclusion, just a lovely voyage, like a trip through the Tunnel of Love, where you pop out the other end hopefully feeling all warm and fuzzy and having added a few smooches to your belt.

Anyway, that's the story. I hope you enjoy the collection.

— Leopold McGinnis

ZEUS AND THE GIANT ICED TEA

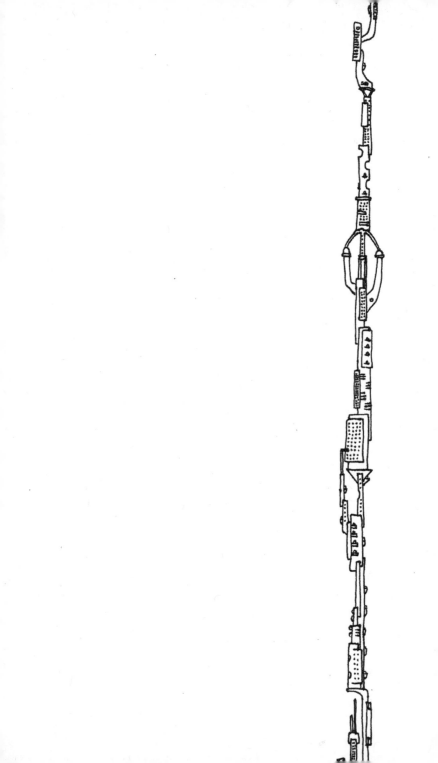

The city

and in a dream
the voice from above said
I can give you this dream
of eternity
if you know
that you can never have it

and before him
he saw a city
of such vast expanse
and vibrancy
that it lay home to a million million families
in a million million generations
all in testament to him
and his dreams
and his dream families' dreams
and their dreams
spreading out
towards the perimeter
of forever
forever growing

and he saw a network of streets
more complex and beautiful
than any spider's web
glistening in the midday sun
with a million million shops
hustling and bustling in place
like flies trapped for dinner
and in the centre of the city

grew an enormous spire
the palatial centre of this fantasy
anchoring everything in place
and on each level
were a thousand rooms
and up and up and up
more than a thousand stories
the dream reaching out
to a sky with no limit
no conclusion
and even though it was so high
that there could be no top to it
and even if you could
ever stand on its ever growing peak
you'd never see the edge of the city
stretching into infinity

And in his dream
he knew that his dream
had built all this!

Then a brick falls
from the tower
in his dream
then one more
and one more and one more
and then a million million bricks
raining down like dust
when a sea of sand
from some unknown desert

starts to sweep through the streets
submerging this spider's web
in dust and dunes
and people frozen in place
become buried in houses
as it all crumbles
erasing years and years of dreams
as if they never existed
as if they never meant anything at all
crushing lives as if nothing
ever held them up
swallowing the dream whole
and stamping it out for eternity
struggling as they might
to keep back this fate
the city crumbles in their hands
like trying to hold onto sand
as if it held some shape
as if it had a will to be held
and him knowing at the end
as it all flicks away
in a speck of dust
that it
none of it
the dream, the tower, the collapse
ever actually
existed

and knowing all this
the voice from above asks

knowing that eternity
is only a dream for mortals
meant never to come true
knowing that in the end
this all will crumble
around your heart
that it is never really there
and never ever was there
would you still build the city?
would you still build the city?

And in the dream
he knew the answer
It was more vivid to him
than the memory of the city itself
Yes, he knew the answer
before the dream was finished
and he knew the answer
as it all crumbled around him
he knew, he knew
the answer somehow
before the question was even asked ...

Yes, he cried,
I know the answer
And it was the same every time
whether the question was asked
by the voice from above
or by he himself.

Robert's Prison

As I was walking
in the forest one day
I came across
Robert Frost
dressed in tweed
and smoking a pipe
who said
when approaching
a fork in the path
he preferred to take
the road less travelled.
And I just looked at him
and wondered
why he had to walk
on a path at all...
Two fucking choices?
That's all?
I'd fall on my knees
and kiss the devil's
hairy toes
for a gift like that!
instead of running
like I always do
into the twisted forest
Stumbling
Sweating
in the midnight heat
of my panic.
Am I running from the owl?

and into the den of wolves?
Or do I run eastward
hoping to keep
the light of the moon?
Or does the moon lead me on
to danger
and I should run through the thicket
the wood's bitter fingers
scratching at my face
Should I turn back?
Shall I dig a hole out?
or climb into the trees?
Robert?
Robert?
Where have you gone?
But the path less travelled
had swallowed him whole
and I was left all alone
in the thick of it
Alone
in the thick
of a million choices.

A Good Day

One day
something happened
and the Reaper of Darkness called
in sick to work
He swung open the medicine cabinet
and spilled all his pills to the floor
Blue ones to calm him down
Green ones to speed him up
and Yellow ones that deadened the pain
bouncing on the linoleum
in a candy-coloured fiesta.

"Death! Death to pills!!!"
he shouted and laughed
before throwing his gowns
to the floor and screaming
a thousand shades of orange
shaking his cheeks until his jowls
blubbered like two bowls full of jelly
and then he laughed because that was
one more bowlful than
St. Nick ever had.

Suddenly he bolted from the bathroom
bursting naked and gangly
onto the streets
screaming and laughing
Showcasing a living garden of
newly discovered bowlfuls

to all his neighbours
he raised his hands in the air
for the first time
free of the scythe!
and then he shook them
and he shook them
and he shook them
like he just didn't care.

And he shook and ran
until he ran out of town to run through.
So he ran through the fields
until he came to the foothills
and he ran through those too
until he hit the forest
and pierced its foliage
like a cannon ball through
the deck of a ship.
Caressed by the needles of a million branches
his rapid-fire footsteps ignited the wild into life!
sending birds fluttering like fireballs
out of the canopy
and small woodland creatures scurrying
from this screaming, rolling, burning, hissing, laughing
ball of ruckus.

But all the branches in the universe
clinging and grasping
could not hold this day back

and Death's wildly flubbering bowlfuls
burst through the forest perimeter.
And as he tore up the mountain face
the peaks and valleys humbled
before his enthusiasm
Death relished the geometrical curiosities
of rocks passing rapidly beneath his feet
and pondered how
that was the nice thing about rock
— you couldn't really kill it.
Not really.

And it wasn't too long before earth
ran out of earth to offer
the peak came and went
and Death launched himself
off the edge of mortal concern and into space
legs still running, arms still pumping
until he hit the apex
of his momentum...

. . .

. . .

before twisting
contorting
and burning back down
through the atmosphere
where he performed a double-backed twister 8 dive
with two loop-de-loops
and landed a splashless entry

into the ocean's saran-wrap stillness
surprising even himself
as he had never taken
diving lessons
in all his life
in all of life itself.

Layered in a thousand blankets of silence
he waited until even oxygen had left him
before he began pushing his way to the surface
pushing, pushing, pushing
until he finally parted the seas
with his bony fingers, making a little hole
just wide enough for himself
for himself and the sunlight
to burst through.

Blinking
into the sun
the reaper of darkness lay
floating on his back
knowing that his pale skin must be burning
but caring little
for all the small deaths
of daily living.

Death just floated there,
lazily sandwiched between
two hues of blue and

wondered why...
more days couldn't be like this?

The Big Shot

Down on the shores of Manila Bay
I am melted into the pavement
with palm trees and pebbles
by the burning glob of lava
settling down on the horizon

Slowly, sinking into the ocean
like an old man into a hot bath
Furious and Hissing
at the close of the day it
boils the ocean in defiance
lashing out at the innocent clouds
setting their frilly edges aflame
screaming
until its face glows red
No! No! No!

□ □ □

Picture me
three months earlier
a white face amidst chocolate skins
in the marbled halls of
De La Salle University
Picture me
in Photography class
— an eager student on
an ambitious exchange —
leaning forward from my desk
...so that the forehead is
closer to the knowledge

My photography teacher says
that a good photographer knows
How to Capture God.
Sure...

                    Framing
          Focus
                              Aperture
          Shutter Speed

...all that matters
but a good photographer
knows God
when he sees him.

Squinting
into the smoky, smoggy
hot and humid
poor and putrid
cracked and crowded
streets of Malate
through the iron-grilled classroom window
he says
I can teach you

                    Framing
          Focus
                              Aperture
          Shutter Speed

...but God
is harder to pin
onto the chalkboard.

▫ ▫ ▫

Tired of the point-and-shoot life
I want to bag me some real pictures
to capture deities in a black box
and distill the essence of life
from the rough ore
of traffic jams and stock markets
Like panning for gold
I filter through celluloid opportunities
for only the best micro moments
floating between the vast banal void
of everyday living:

      An unnatural close-up of a bumblebee;

            A sky curdling grey like sour milk;

         the beautiful orange and brown death
      of Autumn and while every Autumn
is more or less the same
every Death is unique
and uniquely beautiful and
then gone, like a wafer on the tongue,
unless you've got a quick finger
on the shutter trigger
so I never leave my apartment

without my elephant gun strapped about my neck
lest I miss my big shot

Bang!

Bang!

Bang!

□ □ □

In three months I have ensnared
an impressive collection:
geckos frozen on the ceiling
streets knee-high in water post-typhoon
Christmas lights adorning a milky
marble-skinned Virgin Mary
blinking in 35-degree heat.

Now I am no mere amateur hunter
but a seasoned woodsman on Safari
pursuing my right of passage
sneaking into a four-star hotel
for the perfect angle
on a less than perfect budget
today I am tracking nothing less
than the lore and legend of the
celluloid jungle.

Down on the shores of Manila Bay
crouching under shady awnings
ducking behind palm fronds
I plan to pin that burning tiger
between my crosshairs.

□ □ □

Nothing burns more beautifully
than pollution
and it spreads across the bay
like neon paint
throbbing orange and yellow
in the streams of sunlight.

Awestruck before this struggle between
dominance and perspective
played out on international waters
I wait...
and watch...
as the Sun eases its way down
through the burning savanna
until...
           until...
the sea is convincingly molten
and this primordial soup
screams and churns
like something that could believably spur
life into being
with anger and fury

Careful not to startle the scene
I slowly raise my camera

                    Framing
          Focus
                              Aperture
          Shutter Speed

tremble upon the edges
of a half pressed shutter release

Waiting...

waiting...

waiting...

□ □ □

The Sun shifts into frame
unawares
burning, boiling
into my black box
My fingers
grow hot and sticky on the black leather
the light meter flutters in erection
as everything slowly slips
into perfect position

waiting...

waiting...

and then it all begins to slip
through my crosshairs

pica

by

pica

The hot breath of the wind
blows in my face
my vision ripples
and my head swoons
in the heat
as before me unfolds

      a moment

crafted over a billion years
through an
            Incalculable
               Unfathomable
                  Unrepeatable
         series of intertwining events
                    building up
            smashing down
              overlapping
        twisting
              interconnecting
        in innumerable ways from the very conception
                of the universe...

The world swirls in light
and in my mind's eye
I see a darkroom
filled with images of the world outside
like wild animals
trapped in a zoo

I see a life of low-quality copies
rewindable, replayable
but altogether unlived

□ □ □

Down on the shores of Manila Bay
I strip the camera from off my neck
and hurl my shutterbox with all my might
towards the molten waves
lapping at the sand
in chase of glass

The sea in its toxic churning and burning
accepts it with a greedy gulp
amongst the other flotsam and junksam
decorating its lips
burping up Styrofoam bits and plastic bags

They go.

   All the celluloid of students sitting under trees...

   Photographs of children swimming, laughing, playing
   in open sewers on a crowded street...

   Shots of cats slumbering through
   afternoon heat on corrugated rooftops...

an entire exchange
of collecting and documenting
burn with delight
as the Sun ignites the sky in flaming orange

The last protests from my sinking camera
a few photographic ripples in the water
fade away
as the sun disappears
behind the edge of the world
as the sky cools to charred ash
the day submerged, extinguished
for now

for now...

My photography teacher says
that a good photographer knows
How to Capture God.
Sure...

                    Framing
         Focus
                              Aperture
         Shutter Speed

...all that matters
but a good photographer
knows God
when he sees him.

Zeus and the Giant Iced Tea

Zeus lay down
on a cloud
at the end of the universe
sipping an iced tea
and daydreaming
of dandelion fluff

It wasn't a day for lightning bolts
Family feuds could resume tomorrow
And if it weren't impossible
within the confines
of the Greek narrative
he would have pitched himself over
the side of the universe
for a swim in the greyish blue soup
of the Milky Way

Zeus felt sorry
for all those other gods
called on
by their believers
to be Infallible!
Reasonable!
to provide Guidance!
Truth!
Answers!

The truth was
some ridiculous being

gave you a penis
to fuck with
and a brain
to toy with
and a mouth to eat
and drink with
(and you could fuck
with that too
he supposed
if you put your brain to it)
Sundays came
But not always on Sunday
Some people aged and died
Some people didn't...

Who made Zeus?
The Titans!
But who made the Titans?
And what did that matter?
It was ancient history
To be forgotten
It's why people died
after all.

Zeus stared down
at the patchwork quilt
of farms below
and then leaned back
and took another sip
of iced tea

On the Trail of Ibn Battuta

On Sunday Morning
like the great Muslim explorer
I visited the seven food courts
of Ibn Battuta.

And in each court I prayed
at a temple to Starbucks
before riding a caravan of 31 flavours
to the furthest fabled boutiques
of other worlds
and there I Whirled
with the Dervish of Discounts
sat Smoking
with the Sultan of Savings
plying the trade routes
of ancient times
in air-conditioned miniature
where there peddled more merchants
than customers.

Nestled between a handful of exhibits
extolling Ibn's thirty-year love affair
across the Muslim world
I met the Indian Cinnabon maker
the Filipina cellphone saleswoman
the Iranian tie-peddler
while I sucked with Battuta's passion
on a banana mint smoothie
All before lunch

Yes,
I saw a great many things
on my journey.

I saw it all
on Sunday Morning
at the Ibn Battuta Mall.

THE THREE AMIGOS

El Mexicano

He was a mad Mexican
with Gatling guns for fists
And each fist shot a bottle
of hyper-agitated Corona
into the many faces of evil

Yes.
With his guitar
he descended upon this troubled town
and soothed the hearts of angry men
Shaded all the young girls
from the heat of the sun
with his forty-foot wide
sombrero

And what
you may ask
did he keep under his sombrero?
Why...secrets, of course!

Some say in there he kept
a giant bottle of tequila so pure
it would give the devil himself heartburn
Others say he kept the photo
of his one true love
for whom he endlessly scours
the four deserts...
I prefer to think
it's where he puts all

the dumb questions people ask
about what he keeps under his sombrero

Si.
He was a mad Mexican
with Gatling guns for fists
And each fist shot a bottle
of hyper-agitated Corona
into the many faces of evil

He was a mad Mexican
with a heart the size of a gourd
And if you keep your eyes on the horizon
If you keep the fluttering butterflies
of hope high in your chest
someday you'll see his silhouette
rising with the sun
over that hill in the distance
coming to a troubled town
near you

Don't be depressed
sad
mad
or distressed
El Mexicano is coming.
El Mexicano is coming.
El Mexicano is here.

The Two Xs

Dos Equis
The two exxes
The dirtiest man
South of Al Hambra
And North of it too

He was born
in the desert dust.
No woman's son
He was foreign to the ways of women
No man's son
He was lost amongst his brothers

They called him Dos Equis
The two exxes
Nobody ever saw his eyes
under the wide brim of his black black hat
His skin was cold to the touch
beneath his black vest
and jeans
and snake black boots

Dos Equis
The two exxes
He was given a life
without direction
without answers
When he signed his name
he signed an X.

Twice.

He was given a life
without direction
without answers
He was only given
Two Exxes.

The Muscle

Legend had it that
he was born
with only one muscle

his gut.

His head
His arms
they merely sprouted
from it
like tendrils
whose sole purpose was
to move the muscle around
to toss it against ropes
and fling it off ring posts
to wave, taunt, and crassly gesticulate
at the palpitating audience
until popcorn spilled from lips and into the aisles
until crime retreated from the streets for a TV break
until every grandmother in Mexico
was as close to their beloved *Niño Terrible*
their *el Dimonio Dorado*
the *Musculo Antipatico*
as their failing eyesight would allow them.

He was *el Dimonio Dorado*
the Golden Demon
and no one could best
his solid mass

as round and resilient
as Mayan rubber
unmovable
ungraspable
it rebounded
off of everything put in its path
and the only weakness
Niño Terrible offered up
to his sweaty, masked adversaries
was the opportunity for a grab at the hair
which grew more plentifully
on his chest and back
than on his head

The Muscle
was fed on only the finest liquid nutrients
Mestizo cerveza had to offer
Cooked to a golden brown by the sun
greased to glistening perfection
by the finest oil from the fattest coconuts
el Musculo Antipatico
was well taken care of
and from behind the golden mask
came a voice of undying self-assurance
the voice of a champion
and the voice of one who knew it

He was the reigning wrestling champ
from the Summer of 1966

to the Fall of 1969
and the secret darling
of every grandmother in Mexico
who cherished him
as if her own grandson
too old to care for his faults
and drinking themselves silly
as if amorous teens
on everything he had to offer
good or bad.

For it was as hard to tell
if he was bad or good
as it was to keep count
of all his nicknames
but in the ring
that didn't matter
and what else did grandmothers
secretly have to wish for
but the lingering lusty feelings
his oiled up frame
flying about the ring
conjured up in near dry wells
as he grappled
with the all-time greats:
The *King of Saints*
Mr. Whiskers
Wred Fright
Eduardo Thomas del Honduras

On Sundays
after broadcasts
all of Mexico was said to eat
the best meals in all the world
thanks to grandma
None of them even remotely aware
as they smacked lips
and licked chops
and recapped just-finished matches
with open-mouthed foodfuls
that grandma hadn't made those meals for them
and she hadn't made them for Mexico either
He'd never know it
and that was ok
but on Sundays
the entire country supped like kings
on a thousand meals made
just for The Muscle

All of Mexico was in love with him
as if he were a giant metaphor
for something else
and nobody was sure what that was
and nobody cared
but they were sure that it was something good
and that was good enough.

He was the president of Mexico
He was the saint

the father, the sun, the holy ghost
and Judas of Iscariot and the devil
Mexico and tequila
and lemons and tortillas
and everything
everything
everything!
on Sundays

... until the things that made him strong
ate away at him
the beers that fed the muscle
weighed him down
the screaming fans
made him deaf
and the meaningless sexual conquests
stole his charm...
In just three short years
his fame became so big
that even The Muscle himself could not lift it
and even grandmothers grew tired
of giving their best
for someone who never showed up
to even burp or smack their fingers in appreciation
when there was nothing left but bones on the dinner table
They weren't going to live forever
and they didn't want to spend what little time was left
with just one man
when there were so many to pick from
on TV these days

Underneath the mask
behind the muscle and oil and hair
the glamour and bravado and acrobatic flights
he was just another slob
who drank too much
like most of us
and beat his wife
when he was angry
at things that couldn't be touched
let alone hit
who let his dreams
run through his fingers
like sand
until all that was left
was a heap of unsorted promises
that would never ever
draw a crowd.

Once he had been the champion
of all of Mexico
the nation united
under him
Once the streets had emptied
and concrete walls had bulged
until all that could be heard
from coast to coast
was the tinny sound of televised cheers
leaking out into the streets.

Like everything
he was now nothing
but for a brief moment
on Sundays
from the Summer of 1966
to the Fall of 1969
every grandmother in Mexico
had been in love with him.

In the vault of the keeper of dreams

It's run by this old fart
The only guy who didn't have dreams
of his own.
An infinite library
covered in twice as many cobwebs
as shelves.

It's cold and dark
in that goddamned place
and one of the interesting things
is how much repeat there is
categorized under the dreamy decimal system:
miles and miles of dreams about
"opening a business"
"taking a trip"
"asking that girl out"

They say there is another floor
where they keep the dreams
that came to fruition
but I've never seen it.
Is it as stuffy?
Or does the second floor
full of planters
open up on the sky
streaming sunbeams
onto the thousands of patrons below
wrapped in Greek robes
sunbathing and reading

between the marbled columns
unaware of the vault
of dreams
rotting below,
the black morass
of nothingness
on which
everything floats.

The Secret

It was impossible to tell
which of the innumerable charges
drummed up
on his sheet of grievances
were real
and which had been
trumped up
by a government overzealous
in its desire for apprehension
It was impossible to tell
how many tales
of his dastardly capers
whispered in muddy alleys
shared over late-night drinks
in lightly lit peasant houses
were more than just tall tales
for ordinary lives
but between the bureaucrats
who sought justice in unjust ways
and the everyday paupers
seeking righteousness
at the spilling of someone else's blood
on the King's blade
there was little doubt of his guilt
whatever that might be
exactly

We were almost dead ourselves
when we found the old man

tucked in along the mountain peaks
of Pumara Kangur.
In fact
between the paper-thin air
we strained with every muscle
to get into our lungs
and the blinding white light
flaring up from the endless waves of snow
I toyed with the idea that
we existed no more
that we had passed beyond
some otherworldly gate
to a place where everything was erased
direction, space, time, and even feeling were lost
until memory of the real world too
slowly blanched away...
Hong, ahead
clung harder to this old world
marching forward as if pure persistence
could make up for lack of direction

How to catch a man
who'd spent his entire life
on the run?
The government seemed determined
to prove over and over
that it didn't know how.
It was the sun
chasing the moon

And now we were to die
Just another footnote of failure
in this endless adventure
I was easing comfortably
into acceptance of this
and even Hong's stubbornness
was beginning to fade
when the Sherpas appeared out of nowhere
whisking our lives from the brink of neverness
as they had doubtlessly been doing for centuries
plucking foolish mainlanders
from the perils of their own arrogance
Surely
it was a benevolent God
who created these gentle
mountain men

Hong forcefully explained to them
that we had been sent by the government
and they were obligated
under the King's law
to put us up and provide shelter
Though they clearly didn't speak
Hong's language
they merely smiled, nodded
and put us up anyway
in a mountain cave
buried somewhere
in the endless white.

□ □ □

I was with the old man
as he remained one step ahead of us
to the very end
rail thin on that straw bed
as peaceful and certain as the snow
that surrounded the temple
along the mountain slopes

The irony of them happily delivering us
to the old outlaw was completely lost
on the Sherpas
No wonder they had looked on so eagerly
as we supped on the tea and crudely made porridge
they had prepared for us
restoring strength that had been sapped
over days of wandering blind
No wonder they had seemed so happy
to find us in the snow
as if in answer to one of the many prayers
spinning around their prayer wheels
They must have thought we were looking for him
Which we were.
They must have thought we could help him
Which we couldn't.
and wouldn't.

We barely had a moment to empty our bowls
before they urged us up
and towards the back of the temple

into a large room
with a bed in the middle
and an old frail figure
whose breath was so short
it barely lifted the blankets
draped over top of him

Good intelligence
had led the government
to his presence in the mountains
of this region.
But had good intelligence
kept them at it for so many years?
How long had he been hiding out here
with the Sherpas?
Days? Decades?
This old man
unaware of our presence
as we stood over him...
The prize seemed so ridiculous
The government's zeal to catch him...
pointless.
It was a chase that had been lost
long ago.

But Hong didn't even balk
and the next morning
after we had rested
he quickly got to haranguing the poor Sherpas

for a way out
demanding supplies
to make the way
Reminded them, in fact
— these poor outcasts who'd never
asked a single thing of the Heads of State
who claimed ownership over all lands —
that their duty was to the nation,
to provide us with the materials
to enable our removal of this individual
who had likely lived peacefully amongst them
for years
Hong reminded them
that they were as good as criminals themselves
if they didn't do their utmost to help us bring
the old man to justice

My job
was to guard the old fool
lest he escape.

□ □ □

For two days this went on
me sitting next to the motionless man
and Hong's forceful demanding and questioning
the only noise to break up the endless hiss
of wind and snow blowing outside
The Sherpas engaged in perpetual head bobbing
nodding yes to all of Hong's requirements

more out of a desire to help
than out of any understanding
sure-footedly finding their way
through the waves of Hong's threats
like they guided the treacherous mountain passes.
Hong's aggression washed off them
like water upon a duck.

As time passed
they seemed more and more confused
as to why we were here
or what we wanted
However, I think that pretending
to be too simple to understand
our strange outsider's ways
was all part of their hospitality
a piece of the flexible stuff
that made them able to live
in these inhospitable climates

So they gathered supplies
from their scant resources
and catered to Hong's demands
in the outer room
while I guarded the skin
stretched over bones in the bed
all of us well aware
that in his state
there was no way we could get the man out alive

and so were helpless to do anything
but wait and watch him perform
his final escape
Always one step ahead of the law
he was even beating the courts
to his death sentence.

These days were long and vague
and Hong couldn't stand it
He fulfilled his need for progress
by harassing the Sherpas
as if everything was moving forward
as if the snow would clear any moment now
as the old man just took shallower
and shallower breaths
sinking into his bed
eyelids fluttering open suddenly
in the peaceful room,
as if waking from a dream
searching the walls lazily
until those tired old pupils
still vibrant
settled on me...
and then the man would smile faintly
as if assured by my continued presence
before fading out again

I tormented myself
with the question of whether

I should be the one here
at this man's deathbed.
Did he believe me to be someone else?
A family member? A friend?
Was he even aware that
we'd come to arrest him?
To take him to men
who would make him a corpse
and then make his corpse
a public spectacle?
Surely there was someone
more appropriate to be counting
his final breaths

But I needed to give the old man his due.
He'd been at this game
had my superiors on his trail
long before I came along
He must have known.
And he approached this
like I imagined he approached
everything else in his life:
with total confidence and honesty.
Honesty in his thievery
Honesty in his dishonesty
Confident of a satisfying conclusion
and leisurely denouement

□ □ □

On the third day
the old man started
as if from a nightmare
and his hand went instinctually
to mine at the edge of the bed
He was too weak to open his eyes then
only turning his head
as if he could see through the greenish skin
that hung over those now bulging eyeballs
searching for items and people about the room
that no longer existed
living in the images flickering
on the back of his imagination

I was unsure what to do
My heart softened
at the sheer fragility of the hand in mine
but feared reprisal from Hong
wearing his frustration out
on the Sherpas down the hall
as they prepared gruel for our dinner
yet I did not pull my hand away

Later, when Hong came in...
I'm not sure if he saw or not
but he said nothing
staring at the figure there
sinking sinking
into the sheets
Hong grimaced and left

Late that night
it was I who started awake
to the sound of a voice
narrating to me
The old man, looking at me
from behind closed eyes
spoke in a struggled whisper
as if each successive word
were a heavier
and heavier
burden

"Many a man

            wakes

to strive

           for stability
hoping to hold onto his
one............little stake of land
just long enough to perish
upon it

He dreams at night
of fleeing............from the
empty calmness of it
to the darkness and its dangers
beyond. Screaming
at his owns hands
that tremble from the unending desire
to climb the walls

that surround him
on all sides..."

And then he went silent for so long
I feared he had gone to sleep
And yet I waited for more.
Hours later
I was woken again.

As if there were no gap in between
he continued:
"and another man
shakes and trembles
in his cell until
the phantoms in his mind
overtake the fears in his heart
and he scales the walls
that surround most men
runs blind into the night
amongst the wolves.
The envy of his rooted brothers
he has no home
yet no ties
and is in those woods alone
dreaming of four walls
a home
fighting and stealing for something
he does not know how to grasp..."

By the time he came to these last words
I was mere inches from his mouth
as he drained the well of his strength
to the very last drop
just to expel puffs of air
with barely enough gust
to part his lips
forcing the words out in breaks of syllables.
I waited over him like this
until my neck hurt
but he was still again.

Pitying the man
I wrapped both my hands
around his and waited
hoping for this final escape
to be free of dogs nipping at his heels
and leaping through death's portal to haunt him
in a never-ending chase
in the afterlife.

□ □ □

As dawn cracked over the horizon
myself unable to sleep
I noticed that the old man
was gently squeezing my hand
in weak, rhythmic patterns.
I smiled and watched this
wondering if it was the last impulses

of his brain yearning for contact
or merely his blood flow
now stronger than the muscles
in his boney hand
swaying the fingers
in its final pulses.

And I felt a swell of guilt
flow warm into my chest and head
as I realized he had been trying
for who knew how long now
to beckon me closer.

I leaned over the bed.
His body, besides the faint whispers
barely starting through his dry, dry lips
looked as if it was completely inert.
The frustrated effort just to make these last
final effects on the great world around him
broke my heart in a way
no father, brother, or lover ever could.

The sour smell of a tongue
that hadn't tasted food in days
clutched weakly at my nostrils
as I leaned further and further
in chase of his meaning.
My ear hovered an imperceptible distance
above his barely moving lips
cracked and dry

searching out the message:
"I have been both those men
and...I'll tell you

                        — a secret

the secret

                    — life's secret

It...

        It doesn't matter...
    Doesn't matter..."

The man wrestled in another breath and
I feared was going to fade out for another long spell
but the whispering came now again
so faint I was filled with pity
just to experience the frailty
we can all expect
to someday seize us.

"It doesn't matter

                        — what you do with it

because

            because

        it all ends...
                    just the same."

And he stopped there
whether because he could no longer continue
or because he had finally said all he had to say
I will never know.

□ □ □

I held his cool and clammy hand through the night
his breath becoming slower and slower
like waves on a beach and the tide going out
further and further and further
My breath, with it, came up short
unable to break the pace
as if being dragged out to sea
with his fading tide
and every now and then I found myself
suddenly rising to the surface
for a gluttonous breath of air
Those little lungs so weak
and yet still with such power
to drag me in.

Maybe it was from fatigue
or maybe from the thin intake of air
but I was surprised to find myself waking
with the Sherpa's entrance
to wash the man mid morning
Dripping water in his mouth from a wet cloth
it seemed to me that they had
nursed a man into the grave
a thousand times before
and, I couldn't pinpoint the exact moment,
but late that morning I was suddenly struck by the fact
that the ocean had stopped

Only the sound of the wind blowing snow
outside the cavern haunted the room.
The man had grown still and waxy.
He had made his final escape.

□ □ □

Hong shifted his weight anxiously
from foot to foot in the outer room
while the Sherpas made preparations to bury
as with everything they did
in graceful, unrushed movements
Hong, at a loss but to allow this fugitive
his final getaway, allowed the burying
but warned the Sherpas
with much authority
that he was under decree of the government
to apprehend this man
and agents of the State would return in the summer
to claim the body,
intern him were he belonged
in the shame of a criminal burial ground.

As with everything
they smiled
and nodded
and offered us lunch.

The weather cleared
two days later

We were given food and directions
and after a quiet lunch
I packed up my belongings
taking one last look
at the now empty bed
as we exited the temple
into the blinding snow.
The Sherpas watched us from the temple entrance
until distance stole them away
from my backwards glances
and white swallowed everything
once again.

Close at Hong's heels
I made my way down
through the snowy peaks
and rocky valleys
down towards the cities
the courts
and the governmental palace
far below
carrying the old man's heavy secret
home.

Ask the 'stache

Why did he grow the moustache?

He was sixteen
and less than blessed
in the social skills department.

                    (You could tell just by looking at him.)

He was sixteen and much more awkward
than the decent row of hairs
he'd gathered and arranged on his upper lip.

He bagged groceries
at the local Safeway
The one that seemed to have
an ambulance
perpetually parked outside
And for some reason
he grew this plain
straight
black-as-tar
moustache there.

Why did he grow the moustache?
I always wondered
buying milk, bread, fruit.

Why did he grow the moustache?

But these are questions
the world will never address.
If the moustache was providing answers
it wasn't speaking to me.
It merely lay on the lips of its owner
hiding well its small secrets

The Method
(*Wherefore art thou convenience?*)

It was to be his greatest role:
playing the part
of a greasy store clerk
perpetually standing behind a counter
dressed in an oversized uniform.

He believed that every moment in life
should be approached as if a greater part
in Shakespeare's play.
So what
if they hadn't been able to stop
the property owner from turning the theatre
into a drugstore?
Life was but a stage!
So in the morning he rose
and spent an hour in make-up
prepared his material
on the bus ride to his kitty-corner playhouse
and every day he would perform
Living Art
Rolling and Changing those hot dogs
Validating the luck of lottery tickets
Serving the unmet pinball and frozen liquid sugar needs
of pimply-faced teenagers
until the play took a twist!

Oh convenience!
he recited,
Hast ever the world been kist
by more delightful a flowr!?

In the Dojo

In the dojo
there was water up to
the waist.
The wooden dummy
who took beatings
for fifteen years
floated on his back
and the kicking bag
had finally given up dangling

Classes would be out
for the summer
and eventually the insurance
wouldn't cover anything,
the cleaning costs alone
taking Sensei Gnudson,
who had developed an unbeatable arsenal
of organic weaponry,
who had forged a muscle memory
dating back to the stone age,
who had mastered the masters
in Japan, Korea, China, and Brazil,
down for the count.

Who's going to fulfill my unreasonable expectations?

He ordered a can of hot coffee
from the machine.
Even paid for it.
And the tell-tale thump
told him
the moment of final anticipation
had arrived at last.

But when he took a sip
it was just a friggin' can
of lukewarm coffee
from a machine!

"Where's my new car?"
he felt like screaming into
the tab-shaped portal
"My boundless and high-quality sex?
Who's going to tear up all the parking lots
and put in beaches?
Who's going to hold me at night
when I'm sobbing in bed:
Lonely, Disillusioned, Guideless, Pathetic?
Who's going to bring me my jetpacks?
My space colonies and sea monkeys?
Who?
This coffee?
Bitter with the taste of a thousand
unfulfilled promises?

Who? *Who?* **Who?**

Who's going to fulfill my unreasonable expectations?!"

THE SULTAN POEMS

The Sultan's Heart

Don't think you're getting off that easy
little miss
disappearing trick

You play your first attempt
as the wisened thief well
but are still nothing less
than a petty criminal
used to stuffing shampoo bottles
up under her skirt
In way over her head
and running too fast
to know it yet.

This is the Sultan's heart
and you can't just
run your fingertips
over the aorta
admire its shine in the light
then tuck it under your armpit
and vanish out the door
like it was nothing.

Run
little thief
The Sultan won't chase you
In fact
the Sultan doesn't even want his own heart back
He's found one better
he'd like in return.

You can hide in any
of the city's million parapets
the Sultan only enjoys searching for you
his minions will knock on your every door
on every house in every street in every kingdom
his poetry will ring out over the burning sky
as far as the eye can see can see
settling in the ears of friends, family, enemies, lovers
and, yes, your ears too
little thief
his fantasies will slip into your dreams
run a thousand tongues along every curve of your
thoughts
and tickle you awake.

You've stolen the Sultan's heart
and now you know that he cannot be satisfied
until he has been satisfied with yours
in return

In the Petticoat's Palace

In her secret cave
blanketed deep in a desert mountain
she lies, lies, lies
on a million-dollar rug
by the stream that runs
through her candlelit cavern
tickling away not only the heat of midday
that sets down in the desert
like a fat man after a large lunch
but sweeping back too
the demons that would fight
a deeper night's sleep

In hiding from his royal advances
the thief in her petticoat
sits with the Sultan's ruby-rouge heart
in her hands
delicately exploring its edges
as she listens for his army of warriors
now pulled from the battlefield
on all fronts
in quest of the Sultan's new obsession
and at night
sometimes
she can hear the call of his poetry
in its long desperate journey over the desert
knowing every scorpion
snake, rat, and beetle along the way
must hear it too

Admiring her wall of hearts
and other collected prizes
things she's stolen from here and from there
mundane items lifted from the most exotic locals
keepsakes pinched from the darkest dankest lairs
never to be feasted upon by other eyes
satisfaction does not sleep with her tonight

She has secreted too
even the most useless of things
for herself
The shirts off of men's backs
Men from the sheets of other women's beds
Food from the verge of a gourmand's lips
collected here
a thousand things useless to her
but as souvenirs of the act itself

As a girl she never dreamed
of wearing a thief's cloak
but the lust for taking
could not be satisfied
by denying it
And oddly
she now realizes
as the stream dallies with
her midnight thoughts
neither can it be fulfilled
by fulfilling it

for she keeps stealing
and stealing
as if looking for an answer
to a question asked in the crib
but all the answers she finds and takes
are temporary
and disappear like water
on the desert's horizon

And the most prized of her possessions
that has kept her trapped here
unable to indulge in new thirsts for months
that has most strangely satisfied her
above all her mementos
leaves a curious aching inside...
She has stolen it
and even though she rolls it in her hands
every night
feeling its weight, knowing its heft
exploring its smooth marble surface with her fingertips
she is still not in complete possession of it!
The Sultan's heart...
she did not want
but just took, instinctually
like all the souvenirs
on her wall of hearts...
But unlike all the others
she holds onto it
unsure of why it shines so brightly

even after its having been stolen
as if it had never been stolen
at all!

The thief in her petticoat
does not understand why she steals
any more than she understands
why a cocksure and powerful Sultan
would lust so over a petty thief
who steals in search of nothing

But the question burns
endlessly in her cave
Even the stream cannot tickle it away
and her usual approach to quell the burning heat
does not work
because you cannot steal
a question

The Sultan's Epiphany

The Sultan steps back
aghast
at the moment of truth
as it falls to the floor
from under your thief's petticoat
shattering into a million golden
nothings

After hunting you all these months
all these miles
over all those cobblestone roadways
thirsting in all those sandy deserts
After all these unmarked doors
and open-ended poems
After all the fretful, sleepless nights
haunted by infinite imaginings
of you
petty thief
he never once conjured up
this inevitable certainty...

The shroud is pulled aside
to reveal the terrible secret
of the one who has stolen
his love.

You petty little thief!
He cries in anger and in lust
throwing his scimitar to the ground

with a hollow clatter
that fails to fill the room
Suddenly the heat of eight months
of impassioned searching, yearning, and dreaming
is washed away in a tidal wave of pity
You petty little thief!
You steal hearts
because you have none of your own!

In Petticoat's Kingdom

Oh...
how the Sultan's Kingdom
has crumbled.
The city
and all its surrounds
now a foregone desert
where once a lively spring
of laughter and music
of swirling colours and gestures
danced in the marketplace
flourished in this Sahara
blanketed at night
in the sounds of the Sultan's voice
sweeping over the sleepy rooftops
in playful chase
and waking the city
to each dawning day
like a lover's kiss.

Now all have tumbled
The thief, the Sultan, the city
and all its surrounds
from her intoxicating cloak
and into the darkness
where the moon resides
as slumbering King
awake but inactive
The desert sucks at the legs
of this dream

and the decay of history's amnesia
blows in hot and dry
forgetting this land
before its time
before the tale
is truly over

Oh...
how the Sultan
has crumbled
he who passes his days
as if barely awake
and roams the palace halls by night as if
amongst all his possessions
he has lost sleep
His poetry
that flowed like the richest
of purple and red tapestries
over the city's skyscape
has grown limp
and fallen about the town
like a cloak too heavy to lift.
The wells run dry
the castle walls become sand
and the luster of everything
has worn off
Even the historians and storytellers
keep themselves locked inside
There is nothing left to tell!

The city
The kingdom
The Sultan
have become a performance
where all the lines are delivered
but the blood does not flow
in the actors' veins.

All because of that little petticoat thief!
No story in the kingdom's storied history
has ever recorded such a scoundrel!
How infinite
her petticoat
that it could have stolen the universe inside
and yet even this limitless container
could never hold the vastness
of her selfishness
that has now swept out
and descended upon this land
as far as the eye can see can see
like a plague

All because of that petticoated little thief!

How dare she!
How dare she!
How dare she
let herself
be caught!

By Day

It does not yield
anything.
As it once did
Or did it ever?
I can't recall...
Was it merely always
motionless and flat?
a bauble? a trinket?
like all her other prized possessions
sitting high up on that shelf
deep in her watery cave
a pitiful collection
of wishes unfulfilled
through fulfillment
and this heart the epicentre
in her sad little tale of petty heists
Yet here it is just as sad...
even more so
on my perch than on hers
Had I only elevated the importance
of the Sultan's heart
in its absence?
Did it shine ever so much greater in lust
than in ownership?

By day
the Sultan sits
in his empty throne room
where court was once held

Now
in its white marbled magnificence
nothing happens
air grows stale
and even the sound of nothing
echoes
              echoes
The throne has been turned from the hall
to face the wall
and the glistening red heart
now returned to its white satin pillow
where it sat for years
half forgotten.

Oh how I had inflated her
Glamorized
the dexterity of her thieving fingers
as if by their touch
they brought the sun and moon
smashing together overhead
It did not ever beat so
in my grasp
and yet thrived in hers
Did she blow life into a once stale stone
in audacious lust?
Or did she merely wring its passion like a rag
before leaving us both hollow?

By day
By day
he sits and stares at it for hours
as if forgetting the kingdom
and everything in it.
The Sultan owns everything
as far as the eye can see can see
and yet his eye
can only look upon
the glistening heart
now returned to its white satin pillow
where it had sat for years
forgotten.

Beneath

She has disappeared
beneath its size
Imagine!
A cloak so big
it could steal the Sultan's heart
and everything as far as the eye can see can see
inside it
but when empty of all its ill-gotten possessions
she disappears
stolen herself
in its all consuming greed.

Sometimes it's difficult to tell
if she is more than just
a lump of clothes
and often I wonder
if she has a palace hidden in there somewhere
to which she has escaped
But a quick poke
reveals she has nothing beneath
but her inescapable self

How disappointing she was
in the end
after all those many months of searching...
the furor with which the Sultan's heart beat
in search of the Sultan's heart
the lust set upon the kingdom and the city
like a drunkenness

and in the end
she said nothing!
Not a word!
Not an explanation!
She just let herself be taken
into this foul place
her gaze so lifeless
even the firestorm of the Sultan's fury
failed to find its reflection
as they led her away.

How disappointing she was
in the end
after months of poetry
lifting her up on a pillar to the sun
to laze amongst the Gods in infamy
chase after narrow escape after chase!
What a shock to realize
she was anything but
a God!
A child
could have walked her here
and set her in this cage
shackled her to this floor
where we guard the door
and lock the key in a drawer
and then lock that key in another...
...but to what end?

It's as if the chase
across the great desert
and all the kingdom's nooks and crannies
has drained her of desire.

This is not the heart
the Sultan set out for
Somewhere along the way
it evaporated in the heat
or perhaps it was never there at all
but now she just sits there in the corner
deep beneath her petticoat
deep beneath the palace
and says nothing
as if even speech
had been returned
to its rightful owner.

Yet still the Sultan
cannot pull himself away.
He is caught up in a chase
that has ended!
Like a man who rereads a book
over and over
he refuses to believe
the last page has been turned!
And upon every moon's revisiting
he comes down to the dungeon
to see her

as if searching for something...
But she has nothing
least of all insight
to offer
Despite all her thievery
she has but a universe of emptiness
beneath that cloak
and so the cloak just lies there
crumpled, black, and empty
while he stares angrily
neither say anything
before the Sultan turns on his heels
and storms back up to the palace.

How disappointing she was
in the end.

In Search of Another Ending

Although the nights fall
and fall and fall
in an endless acrobatic tumble
of moon over sun
they fail to end
for the Sultan
And though the moon sets
for the sun to rise
it does not sleep
like the Sultan
who spends his nights
following the intricate labyrinth
of golden Herati patterns
painted upon the ceiling
unable to find his escape...

Instead of sleep
the Sultan seeks out his papers
restlessly resting in his parapet high above
the palace's many domes, arches, and ramparts
and breaks pens on the table
when the words become too angry
and the search for resolution too forced
Though the ink bleeds freely
over his hands, the desk
down his kaftan and onto the floor
his poetry does not flow
at all.

And so
alone in his tower high above
as the city turns in to sleep
and sleep and sleep
he takes refuge
from expressions of the heart
in reviewing the words that once coursed
easier than his own blood
that once surged across the cityscape
soaked the desert
and drowned everything in the path
of his overflowing obsession.

Peering down to the swimming pool below
where the garden once was
he ruffles through his sheets
as if trying to piece together
another man's scattered diary
but it is erratic and incomplete
Flipping through pages and pages of poetry
endlessly repeating
the Sultan searches for the ending
he had hoped for
but never wrote
when the passion burned hot
in the hottest of hottest places
...for to write it
would have been
to end it.

So there is no ending now
for the Sultan
peering down to the swimming pool below
from his tower high above
has lost the words to write
his way to it.

Her Return

Late at night
— though night does not visit this dungeon —
when the guards are asleep
I steal the only thing left to steal:
A little time for myself

The Sultan writes his poetry
and broadcasts it across the land
freely
A meaningless thing
that has no value
It comes without cost
and can be copied without care
from mouth to ear
from mind to mind
It cannot be possessed
It can be taken
but not held
And any fool knows
that the sunset's gold
cannot be tendered
in any trade shop

So I carve my primitive attempts
painstakingly
in the dungeon's darkest corner
where no one shall ever see them
even myself
embarrassed by my lack of ability

searching searching
to find the meaning
of what can be taken
in all this give

This poem is for you
Sultan
and you'll never take it.

Where the Garden Used to Be

The Sultan built this pool
for you
before he ever knew
if he'd see you again
glistening blue like a sapphire
far below his panoptical parapet
Day and Night
he looks over it
seeing your naked form
quivering beneath the undulating waves
relaxing beneath the shade of a palm tree
browning in the sun and sound
of wind softly rustling over the city
as I write poetry in ode to you
from my perch high above
your smile drifting up
in a cool coconut breeze
from where you lounge below
amongst your books
and innermost inner thoughts.

This pool drinks only from the sky
and shuns the taste of any animal
two-legged, four-legged, or more
Only you are the key
that can part its waters.
This pool is for you
my dear little petticoat
and no one shall ever swim in it
Not even the Sultan himself

And even if you never come
and even if you never do
The Sultan has built
this pool for you

A Gift for Rats and Spiders

The temperature drops
and the rats and the spiders
scurry for dark corners
when the Sultan's footsteps
descend
step after uneven stony step
into the dungeon.

What have you done to it?
he shouts as he storms into
the dank mouth of this place
where even time dies a slow death
holding the heart in his hand
But still the petticoat lump does not move.
The Sultan's voice goes cold
and the dryness of his breath
sends the sour moisture of this cave
back into the walls

A man who has lost his heart
goes mad
And in my madness
you consumed my palace and all my thoughts
like a fire
licking at the ceiling!
Now I have my heart
and the thief as well
and neither do I want
and nothing is left
to lust after!!

Take this!!
It is useless now!!!

And the Sultan raises the heart
high into the air
and smashes it down
onto the putrid floor
its sparkling pieces
Large, Small, Infinitesimal, Dust
scattering across the darkness
their red light dissolving in the shadows
before disappearing
in the claws of rats
and the webs of spiders

Cold fills the spaces
between the thief
and her unfortunate Sultan
and all the fading fractions
of things once complete
but completely
broken

Time steals back into the dungeon
for the briefest of moments
to see what the commotion is
and there is the most imperceptible movement
from the lump of clothes
rumpled upon the stony floor

Her brilliant brown eyes flare
from beneath the impenetrable depths
of that black black cloak
where only darkness erupts
like two quasars alighting in a cold starless sky
She fixes her eyes on the Sultan
as her ruby red lips part to speak...

and the temperature drops.

The Sandstorm

Beneath the cloak
is a sandstorm of emptiness
blowing furious and cold
hungry for possession
and when the many secrets it has stolen
are themselves stolen away
the storm spills out
in a howling orchestra
of a million grasping grains
to steal and bury everything
for it that owns nothing.

How could such a tiny creature
hold all this inside of her?

And when the city
has been crushed to dust
even my poetry
it steals
All of it gone now
erased in this storm...

Except for this poem
that visits me late at night
taunting me with the hope
of joy's returning
only to reveal
at the very last line
that it too has been stolen
by the sandstorm.

What the rat reads in the corner of the dungeon

My dearest Sultan
You pitiful fool
who should know everything
about everything of value
know nothing of hearts!
That they must be stolen
to be worth anything
We can never truly own
our own
And even when taken
or God forbid
given
you can never truly
own another's
But my dearest Sultan
you should know
Oh wise and passionate poet
that once returned
they are worth
the least
of all

They Tremble

The cooks
they tremble
in the kitchen
nervous wrecks
I have seen them.
Once the happiest chefs
in all the land
with no limits on ingredients
serving the most discerning and educated palette
in all of history's meals...
Now they can do no right!
The Sultan stares despondently at the wall
forgetting to eat
and sends everything back
The chefs have said
it is as if every jar of spice on the rack
has lost its bite
They add more more and more!
until trembling
they cry amongst each other
that it is too much
They can add no more spice...
but still there is no flavour!
The Sultan becomes angry and tells them
the finest cooks in his keeping
cannot make a meal
fit for a criminal
and has them take his repast
down to the dungeon

to be spilled on the floor
before the petty little petticoated thief!
Is it the cooks
who have lost their ability
to find the meal in the recipe
or is it the Sultan himself?

The Sultan
He has sent away his harem
Late on a hot afternoon
he stormed through the large oak doors
and sent them all out into the city
with a sum of money
that would make even the wealthiest
of moneylenders blush
and shut the doors forever
Now they tremble in the streets
uncertain of their place
in this strange, changed
Sultan's land
He has thrown away his harem
and locked the doors tight

The accountants
they tremble too
I have seem them
in the treasury
counting and recounting
smaller and smaller piles

of money
with more and more space
to count it in
as he pours the rest of it
into his secret room
built in the harem's place.
He has hired the finest builders in all the land
to construct a palace
within a palace
so opulent that rumours cannot touch it
and accountants can only guess at its price
from the invoices that flood the treasury
like a tidal wave

And even the soldiers
stoic in their bunkers
tremble from fatigue
as the Sultan sends them forth
on endless midnight treasure hunts
through the castle's darkest depths
prying their torches into the creepiest
of the Kingdom's corners
flushing out the rats and the spiders
from hiding places
only nightmares know of
But in search of what? What?

And for his finest regimental guards
he has pulled them off the front

and set them on round-the-clock watch
of his cherished swimming pool
The pool no being must swim in
four-legged, two-legged, or more
on punishment of the death of the perpetrator
— be it man, animal, plant, or insect —
and all the guards.

The city trembles in the cold
and the thief trembles in the dungeon
The Sultan trembles in anger
And the cooks, the accountants
the harem and the soldiers
tremble in their skins
while the rats and the spiders
tremble in the shadows

They all tremble
I have seen them.

By Night

By night
he comes down and stares at her for hours
as if forgetting the kingdom
and everything in it
He who owns everything
as far as the eye can see can see
and yet can gaze only upon
her rumpled form
motionless in the dungeon
when even the guard at the door
slumbers at perfect attention

by night
every night
he comes down
like a fool
lost in his own wealth
He who has nothing
by virtue of having everything
He who thought he'd play the thief's game
and lost

So he comes down here
and has the guard unshackle me
knowing full well
there is nowhere to escape to
perhaps knowing
though I credit him too much
that this cage is merely a room

in a greater prison
that engulfs us all
and the key has eluded me everywhere
in every nook and cranny of men's minds
Even the Sultan's heart failed to provide it
as it sparkled so in my hands
and now he comes down here
as if I have broken it
when it was empty from the start
and only valuable in a dream

By night
he comes down and stares at her for hours
as if forgetting the kingdom
and everything in it
He who owns everything
as far as the eye can see can see
and yet can gaze only upon
her rumpled form
motionless in the dungeon
when even the guard at the door
slumbers at perfect attention

Now it is smashed
into a thousand pieces
a million questions
as it should be
but he screams
when the answer

does not spill out.
I did a favour for him
for only in its absence
did he burn like me in lust
You have found what you were looking for
my prince
Yes, it is not what you expected
but this is it

By night
By night
he comes and gazes upon me
for hours, silently
as if I had answers!
The childish fool!
Would he not think I'd escape
to find them
if I knew where they were?
Why doesn't he turn to his kingdom
and everything in it?
"As far as the eye can see can see"
There are so many things that are his
to gaze upon
objects animate and inanimate
to speak to
Why does his attention
fall only on me
motionless in the dungeon
when even the guard at the door
slumbers at perfect attention?

The Palace's Story

It is said
that the Sultan's palace
has a thousand ears
and even more eyes
and though none of them see or hear
everything
their mouths bridge the gaps
through rumour and innuendo
as gossip flows like blood
through the most unheard of pipelines

Oh
Misses Spider
have you heard
the maids in the laundry room
all a-chatter chattering
of the gown he's had
the royal tailor stitch?
says the rat
in a darkened drain
far beneath the Sultan's parapet
Sewn from silk so exquisite
even the tailor himself
could not identify it
and so they say
if it were washed but once
the dress would unravel
into a million threads
so it hangs on a wall

with no one to wear it
Who is it for?
is all they talk about
Who is it for?

The Sultan's story
is no different
from our own
full of storytellers
and characters
who never make an appearance
but run behind the walls
and dangle from the ceiling
watching and listening
casually
piecing their own storylines together
from what measly crumbs
our narratives have to offer
here and there

A dress?
cries the spider
How delightful!
For the Sultan's guards
have been trampling through
the dungeon's darkest corners for weeks
carefully plucking our webs
from old to archaic
in the most inaccessible of places

And others have seen them
boiling the tangled mess
in a giant black cauldron
to extract the most delicate thread
man or spider
has ever seen

Even the palace itself
is a character in this one
as it listens to the echo
of the Sultan's footsteps
accompanied
by the tap tap timpani
of the little thief's down the hall
secretly strolling in the sleeping hours
The palace weaves together
a tale to tell itself
from the soft kisses their bare feet
make with the cool midnight stone
as they wander the secret garden
debating the number of taste buds on a tongue
the sound of a thousand thoughts
the number of heartbeats in a love affair

And all the ants are a bustle
on the hill outside the guards' sleeping quarters
consorting with the salamanders
perched above doorframes

Why, have you seen the Regimental Soldiers
standing watch from moonrise to sunset
over the Sultan's new pool
Their gaze is so strict
even the rats dare not swim in it
and the moon wary to cast its reflection
and the salamanders speak
of the secret room
where the harem's den once lay
An enormous hall
bedecked with flowing satin curtains
and tapestries from the finest artisans
a bath and a bed that could fit forty people
overlooked by a giant window
that takes in the entire eastern part of the city
sealed by giant bars for a reason
no rat, ant, lizard, or spider
can decipher.

It is said
that the Sultan's palace
has a thousand ears
and if they could be woven together
in a string
they would tell a fantastic story
somewhere between
half truths
and all lies
like all stories do
like all stories do

He Sees Water in the Desert

The desert
has no water
but these are the words
that I had heard through it
distorted and distant
the meaning muddied and drowned
in its amaranthine journey from his lips
to my ears
so many sleepless nights ago

Now the lips
that utter them
are close
as he rests in his kaftan
against the cold dungeon wall
But when I close my eyes
I have escaped to my dear desert cave
and hear his voice again
calling out after me
over countless desert dunes

These words
are not what I imagined
in even a thousand nights
of ponderous solitude
The Sultan's messages
are much more lyrical
their metaphors and similes
carve my figure in intricate

soliloquies, rhyme, metre
craft together a vision of me
out from the raw ore of lust
love, desire, and determination
The cadence of his voice
flows over my hips
cheeks
legs
and hair
chisels my form
in the mind
from the mind
beautiful and alluring
until even I myself
am drawn to this vision
as to a sculpture in a museum
yet unsure if the sculptor's hand is true
to the inspiration
or if he conjures up a mirage
liars like us
like to believe

And when he is satisfied
with the result
he turns his craft on himself
He builds a palace and a pool
to place us in
Then an entire universe of longing
but still not large enough

to hold all his poetry
all his descriptions of our shared history
despite the fact that we never
shared any of it
until I am happily
but strangely lost
in this familiar but alternate world
constructed of memories
that never happened

Try as I might
night after night in my cave
to assemble this puzzle of drowned words
into the military dictates and threats
I had expected them to be
I never once imagined this
was the message he had for me
Did I ever truly have his heart?
Or was I the thief pursued unjustly
for stealing the meaningless decoy?

These words once traveled
further than caravans
for every ear to hear
Now they are just for
his captive audience
at first in the dungeons at night
and then later as we roam the halls
when no one rises

then finally in his parapet
high atop the world...
now wrapped up
and nestled between
tea and carpets
and odes and odes
so beautifully fashioned
for me and my beauty
or as he has imagined it

And as this love-struck Sultan
narrates our story
in that dimly lit room
I keep my eye alert
for a stray sheet or two
I could slip under my petticoat
They are written for me
but they are not for me
and for the first time
I long to stuff the ream
beneath my coat
to take them
from everyone else
far into the desert
to read and sleep upon
a pile of them
as his voice calls out in anguish for me
through the miles and miles of water
but I stay my hand and instead

lick my lips at the wondering
of what new words
he is writing.

He hints that there may be more
Where once there was an unlimited supply
his pen ran dry as a desert well
But lately drips of drops
have been spotted gathering
on desire's round and rusty spout...
But the Sultan loves all things
in the right time and the right place
and when the reservoir of our past
has been drained
there will be room for new words
to share of our present
But what fun
is the right thing
in the right time?

I am no fool Sultan
You are the fool
who fools his self
You live for the chase
and grow weary
when you have captured it
But for now
I finger the little objects
here and there

I have stolen from about the castle
on our late-night walks
trying to understand their shape
in the darkness of my pockets
as I once tried to piece together
this Sultan's watery words
And I dangerously desire to share
these petty conquests with my foolish little prince
as he shares his poetry with me

But I think better of it.
There is time in plentiful abundance now
as he says
for the past
There is no chase
to be had today
There is only the space
between his lips
and my ears
Between my fingers
and his heart
narrowing with each breath

Oh little prince
Tonight
we are both thieves
stealing room in a world
we long for
but both deny ourselves.

She Leaves a Poem in His Parapet

But even the Sultan must sleep
and the palace rest
It has always been his weakness
There is always one
and that is when I strike
just as I have before
on the blade-thin edge
between having
and wanting

Oh Prince
your heart
was the just the appetizer
that led to a much tastier affair
Rest now
and prepare
for the chase has just begun
The desert is large
dry and foreboding
and it awaits your poetry
with a thirst unknown
Last time
was just a stolen kiss
a quick feel
in a darkened place
Do you know
what true hunger
tastes like Prince?

I invite you
to bring your tongue
into the desert
and beneath my petticoat
to find out

The desert is thirsty
my dear one
Do you have what it takes
to whet it?

Look Upon This with Full Eyes, Prince

Awake
you fool!
The courtyard
runs dry of pebbles
and this thief's aim
is only so good.
Alas another stone
ricochets off the arched window
of your poet's perch high above
and plummets deep into the lower networks
of your byzantine domain.

The pool is beautiful
and so large it would be impossible
to steal
so ornate, heavy, and exotic
it needs no chains to hold it down
No, it merely lies there
bathing in its own serene sense
of invincibility
Just like the Sultan
just like the reason
I stole his heart
in the first place
the fool...

...you fool
the desert heat
hot in the peak of the night
blows cool over the castle

the sound of virgin water
rustling in the evening breeze
trickles over my ears
like a million sweet nothings
and yet you sleep
as I scour the ground
and potted palms
for what few throwable trinkets
remain!

Don't miss out on this one
dear Sultan
We both seek the same thing
and you won't want to miss this hustle
Still the stones
Clack! Clack! Clack!
off the side of your room
and nothing stirs inside.

You are so thick
and self-absorbed
Sultan
you can only chase
and never be chased
You carry yourself
as if unburdened by your entitlement
and yet all your belongings
and even your natural handsomeness
which even kings and princes cannot buy
is worthless

You have a strong nose
and elegant beard
but beauty is still common
like shiny stones
and the glint in your eye
that has returned
to light up your putrid dungeon
is a jewel...
but a jewel like I have seen
in the eyes of all men
when you show them
a bit of this
a bit of that...
What fun is stealing
from the man who has everything?
It is all replaceable.
And yet...

oh I know this feeling well
but at least I
with so little
have the chance to steal it
whereas you started with everything
and dream of losing it.
Poor lost little boy
Your arrogance
firm and hard and resolute
drives little princesses wild
but is cheap and tawdry
before more worldly women
I want to take you in my arms
and tell you how foolish you are

Here's another stone
off the edge of your sleepy nest!
Look around you
and all that you have built
Even in my absence
as you chased me
all these months
you have thrown your money
at useless things
like the forbidden garden
that only the gardener knows about
and the bed of golden silk
and this pool
the only one of your gifts
I really truly like
You are arrogant enough
to lead me around this palace
without chains
because your sense of modesty
compels you to instruct your guards
to leave their watch
if ever I'm to enter the pool...

Sultan...
Prince...
You have much to learn...
Look here!
I have escaped from your secret golden room
My lust has returned
sparked by you

Just as I cannot ever steal your heart
you cannot steal me
Only we can let ourselves
be caught!
And here it is happening
to you again!

Finally
the nimbleness of these fingers returns
as the last of my little calling cards
ricochets off your bedroom window
and slips into your room like a snake
I hear stirring
and your bearded silhouette
charming in its sleepy ruffle
comes to the window
to peer down upon me

You say nothing
as you so often do
and there is just the three of us
the moon
and me
and you
gazing upon each other in silence
for so long
that even the moon gives up interest
and begins to move on
I step slowly backwards
toward the pool
shimmering in the midnight light

Look upon this
with full eyes, Prince
before it is gone
like all valuable things are...

Suddenly
the heat of the evening
is sucked away
and sounds fade as
the water envelops me
And this dress of incalculable fortune
that you have crafted
starts to unravel and unwind
separating into strings
as I swim naked from its grasp
this virgin water welcoming me
with lusty curiosity
I push towards the heart of the pool
smooth and silken
as a dolphin at play
letting you taste
from far above
all that you have missed

Look upon this
with full eyes, Prince
before it is gone
like all valuable things are...

The Sultan Wakes

The Sultan wakes
from his dreams
into a darkened room
wondering where sleep
had come from
and why it has left
just as suddenly

At the window
he stares down to the pool
where the moon silhouettes
and throws rippling beams of light
over a figure peering up from the courtyard
Where are the guards?
he panics at the very moment he sees
that they have left just as instructed
upon the entrance of his midnight guest.

The moon lights up a wry smile
on her face far below
the one he'd always imagined in his dreams
described in reams of poetry
but never saw
until lately
on their midnight strolls through the moon's garden

You say nothing
as you so often do

and there are just the three of us
the moon
and me
and you
gazing upon each other in silence
for so long
that even the moon gives up interest
and begins to move on

And then when we are all alone
in this dry dry desert
you steps backwards into the pool
and are swallowed thirstily
As if at the command of the Sultan's desires
you are caressed and soon stripped
by its million tongues
The dress that was never meant
to find water
unravels and fades away
in the midnight waves.

Your body, sleek and generously curved
ripples naked and blue beneath
the mouth of the moon
hanging agape as he peeks out
from his hiding spot behind the parapet
His one eye opens full
at the fuzzy suggestion of
the truth beneath

the petticoated thief's petticoat
She laughs in the echoing water
and turns to peer up at the Sultan
For moments the three of them sit there
The Sultan without his kaftan
The Thief without her petticoat
The Moon frozen in the middle of its daily chase
Her breasts and stomach
only slightly obscured
Her legs and hips
and lips and all her beauty
leave poetic words dry-mouthed
and swallowing for just air
let alone metre or rhyme
and wondering just what it is
she is planning to steal
tonight

Turning again
the petticoat thief swims
to the other edge of the pool
and hops up, naked, onto the deck of the courtyard
Dripping with water
she walks slowly, teasingly
to the ledge wall
revealing herself
and the creamy glow of her skin
in the moonlight
completely to him

She looks out over the city
the kingdom
and as far as the eye can see can see

Playfully turning her head over her shoulder
she peers up at the Sultan
her long brown hair
tumbling down her back
beads of light clinging desperately
to her shape
quivering in the moon's gaze
before tumbling down
to the watery reflection
of perfection gathering at her feet
She smiles coyly...
then leaps over the rampart
and is gone in a moment!

The moon
caught off guard
casts its light on the Sultan
but does not uncover the expression of shock expected
discovering instead the dawn of a sly grin
gone so long from this land
blossoming on the Sultan's lips
so the moon delays morning
to watch on in bewilderment
as the Sultan lingers at the window of his parapet
following her black figure

as it shrinks and shrinks
into the distance
until her quick silhouette
starts to slip out of even the moon's
ever-reaching reach
and she flickers over distant dunes
and disappears
like a mirage
on the thin, thirsty tip
of the horizon.

Suddenly
as the moon is finally slipping into bed
the Sultan breaks from his ledge
and takes to the spiral stone steps
that lead to his perch
at the apex of his palace
Step after step
to the room where he keeps his poetry
and has called out over the city
these many many times

He halts at the doorway
upon discovery
of all his poetry
ream after ream
page after page
line after line
gone!

And then that curious smile
that only the spiders and the rats
in the dead of night have seen
alights once more upon his lips

Oh you petty little thief!

He leaps to the window
and calls out into the last few waves of darkness
lifting the veil from over the city
that has slept through so many evenings

Don't think you're getting off that easy
little miss
disappearing trick

You play your first attempt
as the wisened thief well
but are still nothing less
than a petty criminal
used to stuffing shampoo bottles
up under her skirt
In way over her head
and running too fast
to know it yet.

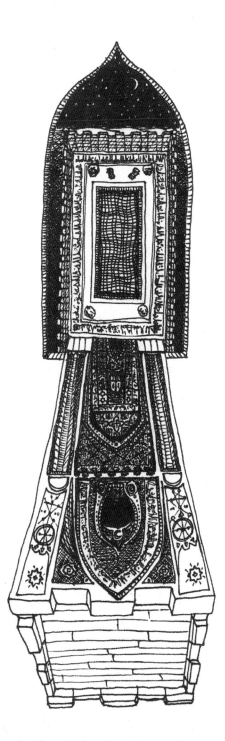

Best Before

For forty days and forty nights
that fridge rattled in the empty echoes
of the kitchen.
The dearth of food in its belly
biblical in proportions.
And on the forty-first day
a loud clang burst forth
through the abandoned house
gas hissed from its chilled creases
and the refrigerator set still.

Still.

Dreaming of the distant future
when its door would hang ajar
by one hinge
and vines would frolic
along the crevassed nuances
of its corrugated interior
when rain would fill her
like a bathtub
a swimming-pool-cum-breeding-ground
for mysterious insects
In retirement but still a thousand years shy
of shuffling off
this frigid coil.

Just the Handshake

He didn't really need to touch them.
He didn't need to see the faces
of those carrying the guns
of those sucking in the bullet.
He just made a series of calls...
Connecting person A
to person B
from undisclosed location C.

He met politicians in fancy hotels
Bought a lunch here and there
Called partners friends when
they both knew they were just
...partners
— not in crime, technically —
but...in shadows.

And he'd put his new friends
in contact with other friends
who were anything but
and together they'd swim through
loopholes
travelling in jeeps over
policy paper Möbius strips

He never saw the money.
Never signed the transaction.
His name would never be found...
He was a ghost

a warm wind blowing favourable conditions:
The politicians and manufacturers
in one direction
The buyers and mongers in another
...not to mention a few excess grains
into his bank account.

He was a salesman without a shop
A broker between people who shouldn't be talking
He used to be a doctor...
now
he made a living
facilitating handshakes.
He didn't need to see the faces
of those carrying the guns
of those sucking in the bullet
He never touched the arms.
He focused only
on the handshake.

The Drop

The baggage manifold
is full to overflowing
but up and down the aisles
the seats are empty

Our fearless pilot
squints grimly at the tarmac
unrolled ahead of him
waiting for the watchtower's call
while the stewardess
is sleeping with the co-pilot
in row 10
her skirt riding up over her hips
as his tongue
tries desperately to rip
a way through to heaven
flicks up and down the seam of mesh
rubbing desperately against the throbbing of her sex

no, no...not now she begs, whispers
when the seatbelt sign comes on
and she pushes harder
against his lips.

The seat begins to rumble
as our grim pilot rolls
down the runway
jolting the lovers
in their compacted embrace.

Rattling, rocking
and assisted by turbulence
his tongue finds its way through
to the chime of fasten-your-seatbelts
and her thighs buckle him in
until the rumbling abates
then stops.

They are airborne
her back arching in the seat
while our grim pilot
curses over the intercom
"Dammit Higgins! Where are you man?!"
But she clamps harder
to pinch out the world
fading, fading below them
and with two fistfuls of hair
she trembles in her own body
forgetting
where this plane is headed
not really caring
not really sure she ever knew anyway.

When the seatbelt sign goes off
they tumble into the aisleway
gorging their lungs
on canned air
like fish out of water
This would be easier

in Business Class
but so empty of challenge
She's slept in too many beds...
Touched down in acres of fields...
Intimacy requires restriction
conflict
borders and boundaries
to be broken and crossed

"Higgins! Higgins?
Are you there?"

But Higgins's heavy breathing
and the hiss from the overhead vents
drowns out room for any reply

"I'm releasing the hatch now..."
the pilot warns
and they climb back into the seats
the swelling seam of his ruffled slacks
pressed tightly against
the fullness of her skirt
as she bends to peer out the porthole
His hand roaming over her belly
they hear the click
and watch the bags tumbling
from the undercarriage
a parade of leather and plastic
rippling in the wind

and shrinking in the distance
A shower of packaged possessions

One bursts open
in the atmosphere:
a daytime fireworks display
of pink panties
blue gonch
orange ties
yellow bras
white shoes
red socks
glasses, lotions, razors, jewelry...

"Higgins...Higgins?
Are you out there?"
the pilot calls again to their empty little world
"Karina? Is Higgins there...?
Hello? Karina...?"
his voice, fading away
trickles down the hall
as the last bag
blinks out in the clouds

Karina rolls around in her seat
grabs his tie
and plants her lips
fully, wetly, perfectly
on his...

Later on
they'll disable the detector
and share a smoke
in the washroom
rolling the clouds in their mouths
sharing silence
and absentmindedly picking at the warning labels
scattered across the little room
later on...
later on...
later on...

The Urn

This urn
ornate and shapely
sits in the back of a dusty barn
among so many other pots
each having been filled
for its purpose
many reused, dirtied, scratched
some broken
some broken, cracked but still
satisfied
their purpose has been discovered
and set
in clay

but far in the back
this urn
ornate and shapely
sits quietly
forgotten and strange
its shape too unusual
to suggest an obvious use
its size too large
its markings too unique
its condition too fresh
to be tossed around
to be filled with dirt

It's as if the potter
in a fit of frustration

or free time
threw practicality to the wind
and whirled together
this dream of maddening curves
and cunning shapes
a useless aberration
to satisfy his own desires
giving purpose to the potter
giving purpose to the making
and leaving none left
for the urn...

Until one morning
in a thousand mornings
that never touch this barn
the potter's daughter
cracks open the giant wooden doors
and comes weaving her way through
the labyrinth of cracked and cluttered clay
rolling, lugging, tugging and dragging
all the other pots
and all their obvious purposes
out of the way
clearing a path towards...
towards...
Clearing a path
through pots so heavy
they would surely crush her brittle frame
if they toppled
towards...

...this urn!
whose nonexistent heart plunges
deep within its voluminous chambers
as her wild eyes and spidery fingers near
methodically...

                  determinedly...

       until...

for the first time
this urn feels the uncomfortable tingling sensation
of his heart rising
bobbing up on something terrible inside
to lodge in the stopgap of his throat
choking the flow
of the scream he trembles to emit

The daughter's hands
a mere fraction of the size
of her father's tranquil palms
whose sure and calming touch
this urn knows so well
grab the thick rim of his mouth
as if that were the way he was meant to be grabbed
and rock him back and forth
on the base of his feet
towards the door

        slowly...

               onerously...

past all the other vessels
and all their collective purposes
as if he were meant to be rocked

And this urn
like all urns
has a mouth
but cannot shout
in trepidation
and cannot ask what task
she has in store...

To fill him with wine
            for the king's seven princesses?

To drain water from a dam
            surely to overflow
                        and wash away the village?

To cook a glorious stew
            for all the woodland's creatures?

No! **No!**
This urn is already full!
with dread
and fear
and even the sunshine
flooding in through the doorway
like a waterfall
cannot illuminate
his doubt
now floating at the bottom
of his gloomy depths

Little girl!
Even at this moment
of long-awaited selection
I have sat so long
I could not satisfy the simple
straightforward demands of an adult
let alone your overflowing heart
though I could easily fit you
and all your little dreams inside
you would surely drown
in this new black mess
that swims within!

Little girl!
This urn
has no idea how
to be of use to you!

But the potter's daughter
oblivious to everything
but the possibility of today
rocks him out the door
and into the mud of the pasture
anyway.

The Big Thaw

She slept in two sweaters
and wool socks
with a Hudson's Bay blanket
thrown over the down duvet
And when it became extra cold in the mornings
she began tucking her bra
into the bed with her
like a lover
to keep it warm for her rising

Then she thought,
Why not my dress pants too?
And next thing she knew
tomorrow's socks were sleeping
with her as well
An entire family of clothing and accessories
until every night
she had a full wardrobe
nestled up under there.

But why stop at that?
she wondered one night
It was really just too bad
that she couldn't tuck
the entire house under the covers
because it got so cold at night
and the bike path to work, too
that seized her nipples solid
when the wind took up
would make a nice addition

Hell, her desk at work
could join them
tucked between her legs
so she wouldn't even have to get up
to ride on the path in the first place
and instead she could use
the warmed-up route
for afternoon walks

All of it
Everything
It could all
go underneath the covers
And while she was at it
the office could come too
the coffee maker
her boat for rowing club
and the boathouse might as well
arm in arm with the little café
she liked to visit for lattes
after those frozen Saturday mornings
on the lake.

Warm in her bed she wondered
why she couldn't stuff it all under there?
make it all her own
instead of the way it was
with everything outside the bed
cold
and needing to be warmed up.

The Failed Experiment

When the two lab-coated scientists
finally gave their robot its heart
it blew its brains out
at just the memory
of how hollow it had once been
leaving behind
only this little data readout
clinched between its
rubbery fingertips

"Query:
Is it enough
to be alive?
Or is it too much
to ask
to feel alive?"

and eventually the two lab-coated scientists
blew their brains out
because in all their years of searching
prodding, poking, and measuring
they could never find
an answer

All Your Questions

Don't worry
ladies and gentlemen
You'll all get a chance
Please don't push
He will be here soon
to answer all your questions
Yes, all your questions

What?

Yes, ma'am.
Yes, our guest can answer that question
Yes, and — what?
Yes, yes, he can answer that too
What? Well... why would you ask a question like that?
But will he answer it? Yes, of course.
He can answer ALL your questions!
All of them,
any question you can possibly conceive
the small, small ones
to the greatest mysteries of the universe
Finally! An answer to everything.
You can ask until your brain has run dry
of questions.
And he will answer them all.
I guarantee that for once
the answers
will outmatch the questions!

Who IS our guest?
Ha ha! Well he can answer that question too!
No. I can't tell you. That's not my job.
I don't know. Nobody told me.
No. Nobody told me.
It's — it's not my job to answer questions.
No. He's — it's a surprise guest!
Trust me, ladies and gentlemen,
all will be revealed very soon.
If you'll just have a little —
Don't push, please!
Please, ladies and gentlemen.
If you'll — just a little patience
and all your questions will be answered!

No. It won't be much longer.
I don't know. Five minutes? Ten? Thirty seconds?
I don't know how much longer you will have to wait.
I'm just the —
Please don't push!
I don't answer the questions.
There'll be plenty of time!
Yes, he'll be able to answer all of your —
What, sir? Yes, I know. I know there are a lot of you
and I assure you he will
he will not leave until each and every one
of you has been satisfied
But... don't push! You'll all get a chance
to ask your questions...

But he won't until — How can you expect him to come
out when you're all screaming and shouting
and pushing?
You need to be...
No! No!
Don't *push!*
Oh no! No!
You're...you're crushing people here!
You're *crushing*! This person in the fron —
Patience! Patience please!
People can't...people can't
they're getting trampled!
they're
If you'll just calm...
Calm! Please!!
People can't
PEOPLE CAN'T BRE —
You're crushing us!
You're
If you'll just wait...
wait...
crushing...
PEOPLE CAN'T B...
I CAN'T BREATHE!!!!! I CAN'T —
PEOPLE CAN'T BR...

The Last Generation

Everyone's talking about the '80s these days
Going back to the future
But I think they've forgotten was it was really like
Or choose to forget
Or were never ever there
in the first place
Because the '80s was just the poor, dusty '70s
who thought it was new
and dressed up pretty flashy because
the '80s thought it would be the *last* generation
and wanted to go out with a bang.

But then the '90s came and the '80s spent a decade
in a depressive funk because its time had gone
Its bang just another stylized puff —
another generational package
of quirky fashions and temporal stereotypes
fading into the past
— or so the '80s thought —
until the end of the millennium
when it suddenly rebounded
out the other end of the
Generational Hole
with a glorious idea

What if it could be the '80s
again?

The Great Indian

The Great Indian
lay in the ground
smoking his peace pipe
and blowing shapes into the sky

The Great Indian
who was but a giant face
in the earth
staring eternally into the heavens
his distinctive chin and nose,
the sharp crest of his Mohawk,
but curious shapes
in the mountainside
blew figures that could
quell the stormy hearts
of even the angriest men:

Rabbits
Flowers
Bar-B-Que parties
Breasts
Giant feasts
meant to conquer
the appetites
of gods!
Clouds in the shape
of every possible dream-wish
An unending treasure box
of gifts for all...

The Great Indian
rested in the ground
puffing these dreams of peace
into the sky with his
pipe.

How was he to know
that people on the ground
spent so little time
looking up?

Crash landing

The plane touched down in Madagascar
bouncing over sand dunes
until the landing gear snapped
snagged in a dune and ripped a hole
through the tender underbelly
of the winged beast
Gravity took its lusty revenge
until the ship slid to a stop
and nestled snugly
in a warm blanket of sand

With the motor still running
blowing whirlwinds of golden dust
up before it
the pilot stumbled out of the single seat
crumpling to the desert floor
and painting the grains
a brilliant, scarlet red
blood that shone
in the sun like wine

Such an offering to such a thirsty desert
which drank and drank
his final breaths until
the pilot expired
and the propeller went with him
some two hours later

Restart?

On a sunny Sunday afternoon
computer games had eaten away
most of the day
and after a particularly gruesome
Demise
the third or forth one
at the hands of the same grisly enemy
our hero turned away from the keyboard
rested his chin in a propped-up palm
and stared out the window
feeling as if he was dying another death
altogether.

A brief history of Gandhi

Gandhi.
He was a lawyer.
He was a vegetarian.
A non-violent terrorist
who walked four hundred miles
in a protest over salt.
He was Gandhi
whose righteous indignation
was stoked in the fires of South Africa
and imported home.

The man.
The myth.
The legend.
When he had sex with his wife
his father died and so
he became celibate.
Sometimes he'd lie down
with a thousand naked women
for hours
willing himself
with all his might
not to get an erection.

Gandhi.
He was a vegetarian lawyer
and he went to jail for his beliefs.
He didn't agree with untouchables.

He thought we should be able to touch everything.
And he wondered why Indians should fight
against the Nazis for democracy
when Indians weren't allowed democracy themselves.
He was a non-violent terrorist vegetarian lawyer.
He was the man
becoming the myth
that would create the legend
and in his spare time
he freed India
by refusing to eat.

Not long after India
was granted independence
and split into two countries
Pakistan and India
Gandhi was shot by someone
who didn't like Pakistanis.
And Gandhi's last words were
"Oh God."

Gandhi.
He was a lawyer.
He was a vegetarian.
A non-violent terrorist
who walked four hundred miles
in a protest over salt
and struggled day to day
with erections.

When he was shot
his last words were
"Oh God."

They are inscribed on his tombstone.

We ♥ Robot

It descended upon the earth
and demanded the love
of a thousand Japanese schoolgirls
Or the city would be destroyed

Of course
the politicians were outraged
Not their daughters!
Not their dishwashers
and prostitutes!
Not their future wives
and concubines!
Not their comfort women
and tea-pourers!
The beauty of that skin
stretched over those kneecaps
That hair, oh so trendily cut!
The pleated skirts
The smoking lips
and fuck-me-if-I-care attitude!
The innocent minds
yet barely aware of alcohol, sex, algebra!
No!
It was an outrage!
It was an insult!

But in the ensuing blaze
of laser beams
order soon crumbled
and the walking toupees

cowered beneath their desks
What could they do?
How could they give away their daughters
to this cruel emotionless beast!?
How could they choose a thousand girls?
How could they choose even *one*?

And as they endlessly debated this
a thousand schoolgirls
gathered outside the parliament
Banging and Screaming
Holding banners aloft
Stomping! Shouting! Declaring!

We Love Robot!
               We Love Robot!
                         We Love Robot!

They were ready to give themselves up
for the future of the city
And besides
they all agreed that
Gigantic Robot was
pretty cute!

And to the amazement
of the walking toupees
and automated comb-overs
the automatic pencil pushers
and subway car riders

the legion of schoolgirls
baked a giant strawberry shortcake
and mailed it to Gigantic Robot
who was so touched
it brought a greasy tear to its eye

And forthwith
the thousand schoolgirls presented themselves
in their long socks and skimpy, skimpy skirts
with their streaked hair and white lipstick
and they climbed up
into Gigantic Robot's chest cavity.

The Gigantic Robot thanked the city
for its kindness
and then looted the entertainment district
for photo-sticker machines
before burning off into space
driven by the hearts of a thousand
Japanese schoolgirls

And back on Earth
the politicians pulled themselves together
congratulating themselves for saving yet another day
and erected a monument to
Gigantic Robot
and the hearts of a thousand
Japanese schoolgirls.

Some Thoughts on Some Poems

"On the Trail of Ibn Battuta": Ibn Battuta was a great Muslim explorer who spent several decades in the 1300s wandering the known Muslim world. Ibn Battuta is also a mall built in Dubai in his honour, with seven sections each devoted to one of the seven parts of the world Battuta traveled to. Nestled, like a watch stand or sunglasses hut, between the boutiques and food outlets of this ostentatious mall (if sultans shopped, you'd expect to find them shopping here) is this little museum that focuses on the travels of Ibn Battuta. I guess that on some level, as shoppers, we're supposed to be Ibn Battutas ourselves...only instead of needing thirty years, all you need is a couple of hours, and instead of spreading the good word of Mohammed, you're helping to bolster the economy. God, I love the modern world.

"The Secret": This is the first explicitly narrative poem I ever wrote. An early version of "The Big Shot" was written about a year before (2003-ish), but I consider it more an autobiographical poem than a poem written to convey a story. Anyway, I had no idea that "The Secret" would lead to many more (and increasingly lengthy) poetic-narrative adventures. But, just for posterity's sake, I thought I'd let it be known that I consider this one the first.

"All Your Questions": This poem was inspired by the "somniloquies" of Dion McGregor. Dion McGregor

(1922–1994) had a strange condition where he talked in his sleep. Not like you or I might talk in our sleep, but all the time and at full volume. In fact, Dion McGregor more or less narrated his entire night's sleep... every night... for the entirety of his life. His roommate, with whom he lived in New York (you can faintly hear the street traffic outside their window in most recordings), became so obsessed with Dion's narratives that he recorded thousands and thousands of hours of the stuff, perhaps hoping it was a key to fame and fortune.

The dreams are fascinating stuff, and three albums (by my count) have been produced, collecting his strangest, funniest, and, sometimes, most poignant somniloquies. As he only plays the part of one character at a time in his dreams (though sometimes he switches viewpoints), you only sort of piece together the narrative of his dreams after several listens. Most of his dreams end up with Dion screaming and waking up.

Completely incidental to this, the two men were also largely unsuccessful songwriters but fame and fortune, though brief, came to them in 1965 when they penned a Barbara Streisand hit, "Where Is the Wonder?"

Thankfully, like all great weird artists, they died in obscurity. May we all be so lucky.

"The Great Indian": This poem was inspired by a mountain peak in the Crowsnest Pass, Alberta, which always looked to me like an Indian chief lying down and staring up at the sky. Lying on my porch one night, I was just randomly thinking about him and wondering what he thought about as he stared at the clouds all day. And maybe his pipe was responsible for the clouds themselves. And maybe, if we were all like the chief, taking time to lay on our backs and imagine pictures out of cloud fluff, we'd be a happier planet. But the chief is a sentimental optimist, and perhaps so am I...

"Restart?": There initially was a second part to this poem. I think it's better off without it, but in case you're curious, here it is:

Day after day...
Pac-Man didn't eat pellets
but swallowed suns
Pac-Man didn't provide answers...
but neither did Mother Nature
There were no keys to collect
no enemies to defeat
or obvious objectives
no conclusion to reach for
no rising from the dead
And though he enjoyed every moment of it
still he mourned the passing of the sun
before turning back to the screen
and taking on one more
easily accomplishable quest.

"A Brief History of Gandhi": Hopefully this poem won't make me go to hell.

It's probably the most facetious poem I've ever written. And I guess that's the point. Why am I so damned facetious? I don't know. But, that said, I wrote the poem just for kicks, and hesitated putting it in this collection — largely because I felt like people wouldn't get it, and I wasn't particularly keen on publicly ridiculing one of the few political revolutionary figures I felt was actually worth looking up to. But every time I came back to the poem, I felt like it needed to be shared.

Why? I'm not sure, aside from the fact that it's entertaining and subversive. But for those of you who might want a more academic explanation, here is why I think the poem was worth including. History is more fiction than fact. It's not written by the victors or the losers but by people who actually care what people in the future will think about the events that happened. And human beings like to pour a lot of hubris onto the things they do. The "facts" of truth, just by the way you present them, can be crafted to create wildly different conclusions. Gandhi was a dedicated visionary whose achievements made an incredible difference in his and millions of other people's lives — and yet look how easily it is to make him look like a fool in a foolish history while still remaining true to the essential facts of his life. I find that really interesting... and funny.

Additionally, the thing I like about Gandhi's story is that it IS so crazy. When I heard that "Oh God" is inscribed on his tombstone, I thought it was terribly funny...and fitting for a man who seemed to make no pretension to his own greatness. Even when he was shot, he didn't bother with some pompous soliloquy but just said what any of us would probably say if we'd been shot! At the same time, his words could have been meant to express his knowing fear of what was to happen to India in the following decades — or at least interpreted that way.*

So why Gandhi? I dunno. Because we share the same birthday? Because I happened to know a little bit about him? Because I thought he'd be the one most likely to forgive me? Because he's so far above contempt that people wouldn't misconstrue this poem as actually making fun of Gandhi? Because making fun of Mother Teresa would just be too much? Who knows. Sometimes they just come out...and I try not to self-censor.

Maybe nobody will get this poem. Probably some people will hate me for it. I'm crazy, and I probably *will* go to hell. But as good as Gandhi was, I bet you he's there too.

A note on *The Three Amigos* and *The Sultan Poems*:

The creative process can inspire itself, and *The Sultan Poems* and the *Three Amigos* sections of this

---

*Actually, my editor (wise to the ways of both grammar and Sanskrit) tells me that the actual inscription is "He Rām," which, while frequently translated as "Oh God," does not carry the same connotations of "Oh no!" "He Rām" is a bit more reverent, closer to "dear God." So there you have it — who ever said poetry wasn't educational?

collection are good examples of where this has happened. *The Sultan Poems*, in particular, started off as one poem — "The Sultan's Heart." But a few weeks later I started wondering, "What would happen when the Sultan got his heart back?" And once I'd written "The Sultan's Epiphany," I started wondering... "Well, what's the thief's side of the story?" Then I wanted more and envisioned a complete storyline told in six poems, which then became 10, 16, 19! I was honestly worried it wasn't going to stop!

The Three Amigos is similar but less strictly narrative. It started off with "El Mexicano," which quickly engendered an obsession with Mexican culture, or a romantic "Orientalist" (South Americanist?) version of it. Unlike *The Sultan Poems*, this series is a looser narrative — I see these three characters inhabiting the same story space, but one that is less important than the characters themselves and up to the reader to imagine.

I've been experimenting a lot with this type of storytelling — where individual poems stack up to create a larger world — and am finding it very satisfying from a fiction-writing standpoint. It takes the fluid, free-thinking greatness of poetry and marries it to the interrelational and immersive appeal of storytelling. In fact, some of the other poems in this collection have since inspired more poems related to them — I seem to have a fascination with robots lately. So maybe at some point you'll see *Zeus and the Giant Robot*...if I can ever convince a publisher to go for that!

Special Thanks

I would like to thank the following peoples or institutions for support and/or for publishing my work in the past: Walter Hildebrandt for believing in and pushing for my work, Julie Ray for inspiration and for pushing me to push myself, Michele McDannold for oh so much help on redfez.net, Manijeh Mannani for encouraging me to submit my manuscript to Athabasca University Press and being very gentle with her well-focused suggestions for improvements to the collection, as well as Pamela, Natalie and Tiffany, also at AU Press, for their friendly help in making the book you hold in your hands look so damn good (and hopefully sell as well!), Richard Olafson at Ekstasis Editions for taking a chance on this crazy poet before anybody else would, *Feathertale* for helping me polish and then for publishing "A Good Day," the Edmonton Poetry Festival for always having a spot for me, Ashok Niyogi for introducing me to India, and ongoing thanks to a whole slew of poets too numerous to mention here for being sounding boards, inspirations, friends, supporters, contributors, helpers, and more in my literary journey.

About the Author

People change
and an author bio
is just a slice in time
In previous bios
Leopold was
a son of academics
a literary activist
and international traveler
the author of one, two
then three books of fiction
and a book of poetry

People change
and writing an author bio
is like trying to catch a day
between two chopsticks

like trying to be
a lover
a poet of immodest fame and reward
Leopold is
rarely on time for work
not Leopold's first name
less stubborn than he used to be
the author of this book.

People change
and in the future
this bio will be outdated
before Leopold can become
a robot with a heart for a brain
a Mexican with a gourd full of tequila
the Sultan of Orientalism
not embarrassed by this bio
a fond memory.

Other Junk

Hey, if you liked this, you can find links to much more stuff at www.leopoldmcginnis.com and watch some YouTube videos at youtube.com/reotord.

Or look out for these other books by yours truly:

Poetry
  Poetaster

Fiction
  Bad Attitude
  Game Quest
  The Red Fez

Colophon

This book was set in Officina, designed by Eric Spiekermann and issued in 1990 through ITC. The other typeface is Refrigerator.